The Wave

Eane Watson

The Wave

Preamble

This is my second book of poetry after 'The Mountain'. As a person, as a writer, I am growing, learning. May that never end.

Many of my poems reflect this journey, and often the mistakes that I make and have made. Many are about love; that strange, wondrous, fickle thing that I do not understand, Others are about life, and death is a part of life – this is not morbid or fatalistic, but a considered explanation of that Great Journey we must all, one day, set off upon... to where and what end, none can know or tell.

This is not high prose. It is terse, often blunt. However, my writing says what it says, no more and no less. My words mean exactly what they say. There is no subterfuge or hidden meaning, it is all right there in front of you.

I have said enough. Thank you for picking up this book, and I hope it gives you thought and aid. I welcome feedback; constructive criticism is what helps me to grow, improve, learn. If you are so inclined, email me (eanegwatson@gmail.com), and I will endeavour to respond as soon as I can.

With regards, and respect,

Eane Watson

7th April 2020

Contents

No Filter	14
Freed	14
Of Leaden Morning	15
Night Water	15
Little Bird	16
Flower, In Vase	16
Among the Trees	17
In Sight	17
Halfling	18
Midmorning	18
Rejection	19
Call Time	20
Ursus	20
Tantalus	21
King	21
Meh	22
Miles and Miles	22

The Wave

Examination	23
Haze	23
Choosing	24
The Lie	24
Hurricane	25
Offering	25
The Gift	26
Lowering, Darkening Sky	26
The Joke	27
Unarmoured	27
Feedback	28
Stuck	28
Open and Closed	29
Daughters of Vellamo	29
Vires Acquirit Eundo	30
Bridge	31
Subsidence	31
The Palace	32

The Wave

Aureum	32
Fortune	32
Lightbringer	33
Candle	34
Art, in Life	34
Mea Gloria Fides	35
Barbarian at the Gates	36
Pages	37
Visitor	37
Fire	38
Space, and Time	38
Unanswered	39
After the Storm	40
Portent	40
Stirring	41
Sundays	41
Foretelling	42
Tyhjyys	42

The Wave

Seer, Sear	**43**
Stamford Bridge	**44**
Café	**44**
Osmosis	**45**
October	**45**
Neither Too Much or Too Little	**46**
Nothing to Give	**47**
Sunday	**47**
Interval	**48**
Spoken	**48**
The Long Drop	**49**
Spectre, Spectacle, Spectrum	**49**
Coffee, The Morning After	**50**
Letter to a Friend	**51**
Awake	**52**
War	**52**
Stasis	**53**
Dust Motes	**53**

The Wave

Achilles' Heel	54
Golden	55
Monkey Trap	55
Tuesday	56
Do as Thou Wilt	57
Garden	57
Sentry	58
Error	59
Thomas	59
By A Different Measure	60
Bind	61
Intrantes	61
Bemused	62
Friday	62
Question	63
Essence	64
Release	65
Thursday	65

The Wave

Once, Twice	66
Monkeys	66
Stone	67
An Aura in Warning	67
Confessional	68
Spinning	68
Empty Hands	68
Silver Medal	69
Load Yet Borne	69
The War	70
Dilution	70
Of Love	71
As I Lay Me Down to Sleep	72
Widgee Creek	72
Virtual	73
Captain	73
Full Moon	73
The Walk Home	74

The Wave

Witness	75
Déjà vu	75
Apart, and Ascent	76
Heathen	76
One Little Pill	77
Unconditional	77
Madspace	78
Prosopagnosia	78
Illude, Delude, Allude	79
Owls	79
Loosed	80
Magpies	80
Rabbit Hole	81
Chasing Shadows	81
I Am / Not	82
A Storm at Sea	82
Sight	83
Rights	83

The Wave

Helios	84
Lesson	84
Ita Fiat Esse	84
Place	85
Too Much	85
Elements	85
East of the Pier	86
Comment	86
Monday Coffee	86
The Wave	87
Relive	88
Lullabies	88
Await	89
Worn	89
Flight	90
Plague	90
A > B > C	90
Stasis	91

The Wave

Away	91
Waters Fall	92
Songs of the Heart	92
Each for Equal	93
Logos	94
Compartments	94
Giving Space	95
Independence	96
Kindness	96
Awake	97
Moonlight	98
Smoke, Fog	98
Fihi Ma Fihi	99
Apples and Oranges	99
To What End	100
Beholder	100
Presence	101
The Living Ocean	102

The Wave

Valentine's Day	102
Kejserens Nye Klæder	103
Suitcase	103
Lucky	104
An Ode to Tolkien	104
Fences	105
Cessation	105
Wages	106
Undue	106
A Waging of War	107
Opening	108
Rout	108
7.24am to Central	109
Muted	110
20/20 Vision	110
In the Old Masonic Hall	111
Salt	112
The Demon Beast Bows Down to the Warrior	112

The Wave

Aft and Fore	113
Fallen	113
Rivers	114
A Rupturing of Levels	114
Breaking the Dry	115
Thursday	116
Freedom	116
Scar	117
Cold Turkey	117
Mit Dir, Ohne Dich	118
Industrial	118
Exam	118

The Wave

No Filter

I've done wrong

Made mistakes, many

No doubt, there are more

Unseen, not yet known

Given wounds, scars

As gravel, acid, knife

And I know full well

For every hurt inflicted

I feel, and reap, tenfold

Freed

To be free is not

To face fear

But to pursue it

As a hunter

Seeks its prey

To wrestle, grapple

Seize, and hold, death close

The Wave

Until you see, know it

For what it is

Life, beyond life

Of Leaden Morning

The morning erodes

Out of naught

Grey, washed from black

An unlight in the sky

I, alone, can see

The ash falling

Drifting

Night Water

Swirling, of all

Shades of black

The silent current

Bleeding, devouring

Seeping into my soul

The Wave

My heart, my eyes

The colour of the void

Little Bird

I can see her beauty

Gentle, and sunlit

Breathe it in

And let it go

Flower, In Vase

We cut the stem

The beauty, and life

Which we sought

To possess, is thus

Destroyed

The Wave

Among the Trees

Something black

Not in colour

But substance

On the edges

Of sense, and sight

Turning, teeth bare

I became its hunter

And it fled

Into the nothing

In Sight

The signs, and their absence

Are plain to see

For those willing, able

To read, trace them

Let it all fall away

The currents deep of the will

Beneath swirling winds of fate

The Wave

Halfling

I have sought only pleasure

Fleeting joys, vanities

Of spirit, and flesh

Yet spurned, hidden from

Pain, discomfort, the cold light

Of failure, and failing

This is not wrong

But it is incomplete

All should be sought

Lived in, lived through

Seen for what they are

Tests, and trials, of the Gods

Midmorning

A movement of the air

In the stillness, and heat

Sudden moment of silence

Amongst the traffic and noise

The Wave

It is the changes

That we sense, feel

Yet it is the vastness

Of the complete, eternal

That which does not shift

Is which we must seek

Rejection

However kind the knife

The wound which gapes, burns

Eating away, an acid hurt

Etching into the soul

Questions, doubts of worth

The mirror unkind

Measured on the scales

And being found wanting

Against another, or nothing

The Wave

Call Time

Spent and worn

I shut the door

To everyone, everything

Nothing more to give

Except love, and care

Yet those things

Too, are wasted

Ursus

It is a day of change

The truth stirs within

Awakens, shifting, breathes

Beneath skin, within soul

What is man, what is not

Becomes unclear, uncertain

The Wave

Tantalus

No nectar nor ambrosia

Did I from the table steal

Pelops, safe from my hand

Yet, I too, reach

For fruit beyond my grasp

The waters receding

My thirst, unquenched

King

For aeons, have I waited

For the dawn

Suspended as I am

In the dark

The void above, below

Beside me

No, in majesty, I know

I, the sun

The Wave

The fire, promethean
Mine to give
Flooding cold abysses
With love, with light

Meh

I am only
What I am
And that will
Never change
Not enough
For you
It is enough
For me

Miles and Miles

Every time
I see that face
That feeling again

The Wave

Something without words

But also, the distance

Here, but out of reach

Examination

Every moment

A test of purpose

Will you succumb

Or will you be true?

Haze

The sun burning

Arising, in smoke

And ash, flame

Heralds the summer

The Wave

Choosing

To love, yet be unloved

They shake their heads

Tell me to close the door

And walk away

To stay begets pain

Yet I do not, will not

To me, the will

To love, being unloved

Remaining, with open heart

Asking, and expecting, nought

Is to grow, stay true

To live beneath the sun

The Lie

If not living

Your truth

What then

Are you living?

The Wave

Hurricane

Why cower, hide, from the storm

When you can embrace its fury

Dance with the winds

In awe of its lightning

Rejoice, for such power, grandeur

A rare and wondrous thing

Its destruction begets creation

New growth, and life

The rotten and the dead

Boldly swept away

Offering

What do I have

To give, to offer

Only myself

No bright lights

Fame, nor fortune

Little by way of charm

The Wave

Of no pedigree

Unhandsome

I simply am here

A full heart

And empty hands

The Gift

I give freely

Even knowing

It is only set aside

Given in turn

To another

One who is

Not I

Lowering, Darkening Sky

I see the coming storm

Hear the thunder

Feel the lightning

The Wave

Taste the rising wind

Sniffing the god-scent

The bear spirit within

Stirs, awakens

The Joke

The wanton, fickle Gods

Have placed the sun

Within my reach

Yet not within

My grasp

Unarmoured

I will gladly face the foe

Give, receive the wounds

Rejoice with no quarter given

Stand, endure, conquer

Yet the things that bring me low

The subtle poison of words

The Wave

Time's millstone grinding

This aching of the heart

Feedback

To disown my thoughts

Deny the content, substance

Of my heart and being

Is folly, madness

The path of a coward

I cannot be less

Than true, sincere

Unconcerned by consequence

Stuck

Caught between

Moving forward, on

Pulling, stepping back

Staying right here

Wanting all, one

The Wave

And none

Open and Closed

Neither wondering why

Nor knowing

Changes anything

It is what it is

No action

Or absence thereof

Shifts realities

Daughters of Vellamo

They are as the ocean

Wild, majestic, free

Unable to be contained

Predicted, or owned

Many will baulk

On the dunes

At the winds, and squalls

The Wave

Some will shiver

At water's edge

Closed, confused, afraid

But who of you

Will with me

Plunge into the waves?

Vires Acquirit Eundo

Far better to live

Heart opened to life

To be free

Whether in joy

Or in pain

Than to close it

Death, until death

I open wide my chest

To the world's barbs

That arrow lodged deep

I endure, I stand

The Wave

I set myself free

Bridge

Your words

Say one thing

Your deeds

Another

Subsidence

Questions only exist

Within hearts, minds

Answers and truths

Never need to be

Found, created

They simply are

To be realised

Accepted

The Wave

The Palace

Whenever I seek

To close the door

Windows to shutter

She laughs

Flooding the room

With light, with air

Aureum

I want to kiss you

But your heart

Is over horizons

You do not see me

Fortune

The cards before me

Speak of toil, of strife

A war without end

The Wave

Paths walked alone

Of reward, repayment

Not found in this life

But in another, beyond

This, I welcome

My fate and my will

I master, rejoicing

In the battle

Its own wage

Under these signs

Shall I conquer

Lightbringer

All comes at a cost

Creation, from destruction

Compromise erodes

Devours the soul

Until nothing is left

And nothing

Can them be saved

The Wave

Candle

Light the flame

Tend it close

It may not be

For your fire to set

It may just be

To help another

Fan theirs

Art, in Life

Right there before me

A portrait of beauty

Majesty, and strength

Such things can never

Be owned, possessed

Nor should they

Be hidden away

Guarded jealously

But beheld, admired

The Wave

For such as they are

Mea Gloria Fides

Renown won, earned

Faith kept, fealty

Vain-glory at best

Whether in vanguard

Or rear-guard, to fall

When few will stand

Yet far better to hold

Fast, until end bitter

Pierced by darts

Of foe, and friend

Than to betray, break oath

Or to safety flee

A traitorous cur

Give me death brutal

Over life disloyal

The Wave

Barbarian at the Gates

I wander the city

Halls, and houses

Among men, polished, smooth

Their wit, and charm, clever

Gilded facades smiling

I am curious, and not

As to what lies beneath

I am sure their gaze

Upon me is disdain

As much as mine

In return, indifferent

Give me instead

The purity, truth

Of hill and stream

Solitude of the woods

The Wave

Pages

Pages yet empty

Waiting, the pen poised

Every word, a footstep

Each line, a story

A chapter, a lifetime

Visitor

For a moment, she was there

White, wreathed in white

Her ageless countenance

A gaze serene

I know not why she appeared

At my window

In the depths of night

An omen, a portent, herald

Spirit wandering

Our eyes met, for a moment

And she was gone

The Wave

Darkness, wreathed in darkness

Fire

Pile the timber high

The kindling lay

Yet if the flint

Can strike no spark

There will never be

A flame

Space, and Time

There is a pattern here

A continuum, a spiral

Looping upwards, and down

To be broker, or yet

Followed, to what end?

Answers to be found

Within, and without

Mostly in the between

The Wave

To cut myself loose

Or to hold on, in hope

Better yet, to be

Immerse myself in waves

Know them, and their parts

Allow time, and space

What will be, will be

Unanswered

When words spoken

Are heard

And written, seen

Without reply

Such things

Themselves

Are answers

The Wave

After the Storm

The crescendo of rain

Ceases abruptly

A sudden silence

Louder than noise

Leaden clouds eroded

By moonlight

Portent

After the night

Unrestful sleep

Full of war, fury

Unnamed horror

I care not describe

The raucous crows

Beyond my window

Drew me to the surface

Sucking in the air

Able to breathe again

The Wave

Clearing away wrath

From my veins

Stirring

Cold and strong is the wind

The clouds blessing the Earth

I yearn for the ocean grey

Tiller in my hand

Salt-spray on my brow

An eye on the horizons

As the waves rise

In greeting

Sundays

Coffee and breakfast

Herds of lycra-clad

Middle-aged men

And their faithful

Bicycle steeds

The Wave

Foretelling

Despite lowering

Darkening skies

The leaves are sunlit

Winds blow warm

A distant crow calls

It will be a day

Not unlike today

When my heart slows

And breathe ceases

My toil complete

The wages, I will

Receive, and depart

But not soon

And not yet

Tyhjyys

Errors, mistakes

Seek the sun

The Wave

Pages turn, empty

Imbued with meaning

I cannot put into words

As much as I would

Try to deny, push it aside

It surfaces again, again

Answers, I have none

Seer, Sear

It's a night

For avoiding the crowds

Avoiding everyone, really

Turn it off, put it down

Look only within

To the origin, source

Of the issue

The Wave

Stamford Bridge

Laughter in my heart

I stand alone, tall

Over those arrayed before

Forty shall come, and fall

Upstream the water clear

Washing into crimson

None shall bear my wrath

Laughter in my heart

The Valkyrie descends

I am brought low

Not by those who face me

But by one beneath

Café

Old men talking

Of things enduring

More years than I've lived

The Wave

Slow sunshine creeps

Osmosis

Thoughts come slow

And the words

Yet to form

Let alone live

The question

Is no beginning

Nor the answer the end

They are merely

Stones on the trail

The path its own

Destination

October

The sky has descended

In light and in shadow

All the way to earth

The Wave

Neither Too Much or Too Little

I am exactly where I am

Where I need to be

Precisely myself

For good, for ill, for all

Currents shift and turn

Change, this way and that

Action and reaction

Both fated by the Gods

And gifted with free will

Though the lessons are complex

In their simplicities

The mysteries opaque

I will strive, and work

All will become clear

All will be well

As it was, and is

For I am but one of many

A speck of a firmament

Vast, and eternal

The Wave

Nothing to Give

Uncertain, unsure

Self-plagued

By doubts

Make the bed

The dishes clean

Sweep and mop

Breathe the air

Sunday

I never said that

I was a saint

Yet I do not

Believe in sin

Errors and mistakes

Indeed, learnings

Yet even the darkest

Only contrasts

The brightness of the light

The Wave

Evil exists only
In hearts of man
Intertwined with
Salvation

Interval

Nothing speaks louder
In speech, or song
Through sunlit trees
Than silence

Spoken

The words float
On the surface
Upon currents
Of hidden
Meanings, intentions

The Wave

The Long Drop

To stand on the cliff's edge

One can be crippled

Paralysed by the abyss

Turn away in fear

Or leap into the chasm

It does not matter

If I reached the other side

Or fell to ruin

Into the void

It matters

That I leapt

Spectre, Spectacle, Spectrum

The words are slow to come

Where they come at all

Or even, at times, exist

Rites, rituals, traditions

To master, control the chaos

The Wave

Bring order to confusion

When sight, sound, perception

Floods, and overwhelms

Nothing is then seen

Or perceived

The subtleties of language

Of the face, posture, movement

Beyond comprehension

I have sight, yet am blind

The geas, laws, customs

Of my soul, alien

And yours, I am yet

To understand

Coffee, The Morning After

Laughter, and chatter

The traffic hums

Beyond, trees and sunlight

Washed by sudden breeze

The Wave

How strange, and perfect

Is it all

Here, and now

Letter to a Friend

Hello, my friend

I wish you well

For you to know

Rough seas, waves

For you to master

Nights dark, and cold

In which to know courage

Warfare and strife

To earn victory

Being lost in wilds

And find, know your way

But know, my friend

You will never be alone

I am always here

The Wave

By your side

And love you

For all that you are

Awaken

I awoke to a dappled sky

Its soft, fierce glow

Through leaf and limb

Listening to the world

Breathing as one

With the Earth

War

The assault

Of scorn, disdain

I can withstand

Yet kindness

An arrow

Punching through

The Wave

My chest

Stasis

Unable to move forward

Unwilling to pull away

I float in this ether

Governed by laws, mores

Forms, functions, dimensions

Beyond my understanding

All I know is that

Which is, which is not

And that I shall

Always be here

Knowing my place

And purpose

Dust Motes

So, here we are

Here, I am

The Wave

Having spoken

More statement

Than query

Knowing already

The answer

Achilles' Heel

Sew shut my heart

Transmute it

To lead, or better

Yet stone

Weld close the gap

In my armour

But I cannot

Thus, am I left

With a thing

Without worth

To those who I

Am careless enough

To show

The Wave

Golden

I know of love

The room lights up

With their coming

Seeing their face

A pang of the heart

The sunlight in their hair

A smile, laughter

Are things indescribable

Where words fail

And there are none

It can only be described

By silence

Monkey Trap

Doomed, snared

In refusing to let go

Grasping at straws

Butterflies of the mind

The Wave

Tripping, falling

Trying to reach

What is out there

The mirage

When reality

Is here

In the centre

Centred

Tuesday

I came home

Swallowed the pill

Slept as if dead

Waking into pale dawn

Of clear sunlight

And distant disquiet

The Wave

Do as Thou Wilt

We have been

Cut off, removed

From passion, and thus

From mastery

Of ourselves

Thraldom in freedom

Quietly, slowly

Has the net drawn tight

Curtailing, preventing

Love through to hate

Laws and commandments

Morals, values, mores

A noose on the neck

Of our souls

Garden

Seeds of doubt

Already sown

The Wave

Now flower

Tended closely

By my foes

It is strange to me

As one without

Enmity, or hate

To face such things

In another

Sentry

Night fades slowly

Into dawn

Lightening sky

Heralds the end

Of my watch

Until darkness descends

Once again

The Wave

Error

I found myself judging

Criticising another

When on reflection

Have I seen, see

The same faults, error

Selfish, and thoughtless

Within my own self

I can cast no stones

Let alone cast the first

But I can learn

To be better

And better myself

Thomas

The mirror betrays

Accuses, sneering

The doubt permeating

A dark fog unseen

The Wave

But no less real

Questioning worth

Value, and place

Only finding questions

Whispered from the void

By A Different Measure

He spoke

Said you and I

Are the same

No, I said

I am not you

And you

Are but a shadow

Of me

I am a God

Come into human flesh

A king without crown

The paladin singing

At Roncevaux

The Wave

I am a man

Like you

But our measures

Are not the same

Bind

I could carve the runes

Bury them in secret

Speak the words

Into the silence profound

But I will not

Such power best used

When cast aside

Forgotten

Intrantes

The world burns

Flames of the mind

Heat and smoke

The Wave

Stinging the eye

Nostrils flared

And teeth bared

I walk into

The day

Bemused

The wind scatters

The pages

My thoughts

This way, and that

I let them go

Watch them

Swirling like leaves

Friday

I learnt a lot this week

Much I already knew

Deconstruction of self

The Wave

My place, my worth

A king without throne

Nor realm

I close my door and heart

Walk towards tomorrow

Question

I have not the words

To write, nor speak

None exist to describe

The heart or the mind

Perhaps it is best

That such things remain

Hidden, and secret

So none may know but I

Yet it burns

A mute yearning to sing

The Wave

Essence

Love is a spectrum

Of all colour

Extending, pervading

The eight directions

Ever shifting, changing

Breadth, depth, intensity

I love, yet can not

Be loved the same

Love is, is not a choice

I choose happiness

Anger, despair

Love is all

The very fibre

Of my soul

The Wave

Release

I'm not giving up

Instead, choosing

To let go of things

That I have not

The people who

Do not want me

What, and who

I am not

The burdens I hold

Chains that I grip

One, by one

Fall away

Thursday

A new day

Skies unchanged, eternal

I feel the change

Amidst the unchanging

The Wave

In the eternal

My self, dissolving

Fading like smoke

Once, Twice

When is a fool

Not a fool

Wisdom attained

Or fool eternal

I speak, write

The words

Their foolishness

For all to see

Monkeys

The ink still wet

Yet my mind

Has leapt again

From this tree to that

The Wave

Squabbling with itself

Endless chattering

Stone

I know what I want

Yet I am struck dumb

Where to go

Yet my feet stay still

What is doubt, but fear

By another name?

An Aura in Warning

The grinding

Stone, against stone

A sickly halo

Blurring, blinding

Clenching jaw

Stomach churn

Seeking silence

The Wave

And the dark

Confessional

I took breathe and spoke

The crime not mine

Guilt, shame, nonetheless

The air now cleansing

Spinning

When the swirls

And the mind

Spin counter

Stop, for a moment

Empty Hands

This is what, all

That I have

Sword of spirit, mind

The Wave

Giving life, light

In one stroke

And takes with another

Silver Medal

Second place, choice

Second best, option

The measure of worth

Makes the difference

Hail to those

Earning the fold

Standing in the sun

Load Yet Borne

Wrought iron and vines

Soft flutter of wings

Sun-shadowed leaves

A breeze, zephyr

Cannot still this

The Wave

Racing mind
Unquiet heart

The War

Traps and snares
Will ever be set
Ambushes laid
Battles joined

Though the press
Is close, and thick
Heed the rally
That clear command
Fight through, fight through

Dilution

The old Gods remain
Hidden and cunning
Their power witnessed

The Wave

Wind through bough

Wave upon shore

Sun on stone

As confused is man

With token supplication

To a cross, or crescent

Feeble attempts to smother

Deny what is

Beauty, and the deep

Remains, endures

Of Love

It cannot be forced

Or demanded

A two-way street

Four dimensional

One can love

Yet no be in love

It is effortless

The Wave

In its being

As I Lay Me Down to Sleep

I might not wake tomorrow

One day, I won't

What will remain

Where will I have gone

Leaves on the forest floor

Widgee Creek

I stood on the bridge

Clean stream below

Air cool and clear

And I remembered

The crumpled car on the bank

Broken glass, and the man

Who could have been asleep

If you didn't look close

The Wave

Virtual

A frantic, desperate

Escapism, only pulls

The chains tighter

Bonds with no locks

But the hands

That grip them

Captain

Mastery is not

Calling forth the tide

Or letting the gales

Take you where they may

And yet, it is both

Full Moon

A circle complete

Calling forth

The Wave

What is hidden

The Walk Home

Under bright moon

I left the world of man

Trod darkened lanes

Through tree and mist

Where dwell the others

At the edges of sight

And of hearing

Beneath limb and leaf

In waters dark, deep

They knew me, and I them

The spirits, and the Gods

I entered again

The world of man

Under pale streetlight

Once again, alone

The Wave

Witness

I will bind myself to the stone

And stand, thus, and fall

I am uncaring if my name

Is known, remembered, forgotten

By mortal men

The Gods shall witness

And I shall walk beyond

Déjà vu

I've been here before

In this moment

Yet I recall nothing

Still learning the lessons

By rod, and by rote

Until it all dissolves

The moment ceases

And never was

The Wave

Apart, and Ascent

I do not know

What you want

Only that it is

Not I, not me

I know what I want

The higher, regal, pure

That which shines

Among the dust

Heathen

Your God is not mine

The laws of fire and blood

Carven into stone

Alien to me

No desert daemon I follow

I will not speak to you

The Wave

Of my ways, my geasa

The things woven into me

For they are

As alien to you

One Little Pill

I can feel it rising

The burning waters of Odr

It is not yet mastered

The work still incomplete

I cannot take my place

Among the Ulfhednar, Svinfylking

My Hamrammr unearned

Unconditional

I don't need to know

Who you're with

What you're doing

When you'll be back

The Wave

Where you are

Or why

I want to know

That you're safe

Happy, and well

Madspace

And with that the waves subside

No urgent winds now blow

The ache of weariness

A burden released

The new day's dawning

Prosopagnosia

It has its advantages

You seem new

Different

Wonderful

The Wave

Every

Single

Moment

Illude, Delude, Allude

The black picket fence

Astroturf green

Seems to sum up existence

Which half of the coin

Is which?

Owls

Here we are again

Another morning, coffee

What is there to be said

That has not yet been spoken

By the time I figure out

The swirls in my mind

The Wave

You, and the morning

Will be gone

Loosed

I spoke the words

And I wonder, did I err

Yet the arrow has flown

I cannot stop its flight

Magpies

Complexity of birdsong

I listen unknowing

Yet I wager

It knows nothing

Of the follies

Of humankind

The Wave

Rabbit Hole

Answers beget

More questions

To what end?

Until realisation, awakening

That there are no answers

Nor questions

Chasing Shadows

To not know

Is to opine, believe

Standing on sands

A chasing of ghosts

Illusion, delusion

The Wave

I Am / Not

The smartest man

Stronger than all

Wiser than you

Compassionate, kind

One to make you laugh

The warder of the night

Everything, and none

A Storm at Sea

Stepping away from the lights

Song, and revelry

I went forward, on the bow stood

Beneath the thunder

Lightning flash revealing

Hills of water, advancing

In between – the abyss, darkness

In an eternal moment

There were no Gods

The Wave

No sky, horizon

In the emptiness, everything

As nothing, as one

Sight

I can see what is now

What is yet to come

A loss, turning away

And a new direction

Rights

You cannot ask for what

Has not been earned

In the work

Is the wage

Sweat transmutes to gold

The Wave

Helios

Galileo, Aristarchus

One step further

Firmament vast

Among the infinite

I am but one

Lesson

Time again, learning

As the hammer

Drives nails into wood

Ita Fiat Esse

I can only ask the question

Open the gate, and wait

The true, truth unconditioned

Unforced

I will not ask for other

The Wave

Place

I know what I am

Who, where and why

My purpose, place, direction

Looking within, without

Above, and below

Too Much

Lying awake thinking

Of thinking

About thinking

Elements

Stillness in movement

Everything breathes

Nothing, and all things

Are significant

All things, and nothing

The Wave

Matter at all

East of the Pier

At the edges

Of grass and sand

Above the water

Stretching beyond horizons

Comment

I say too little

This is true

Preferring instead

To watch, listen

Dissect, examine, understand

Monday Coffee

Sitting, watching

Within, yet apart

The Wave

Ebb and flow

The endless moment

As still as

Streams running

Turning skies

The Wave

The wave rose

You and I as well

The swell lifting us

Together

The skies drifted down

Freshwater on salted

Our faces upturned

Our footprints

Wet sand, dry

Fading, yet

Forever remain

The Wave

Relive

I know how this ends

We've been here before

The same patterns, currents

Yet different actors

The wheel turns

Until it's broken

Lullabies

As a child, the night

And its silence

I knew only as

Undertoned, in distance

The doomsday rumble

Of factory, machine

Tinged in early hours

By sombre klaxon blare

The Wave

Await

I lie down

Back on grass

Eyes to stars

Wondering

When will I return

Flesh to soil

Spirit above

Worn

There is so much

I want to say

Yet it's all been said

Time, and again

The millstone-groove

In circle carved

The Wave

Flight

A bag by the door

Leaving for need

Wanting to stay

My heart here

As well as there

Plague

I, virus

Fuck and consume

Cover the earth

With artefacts

Mindlessly

A > B > C

I'm in trouble

She said

So am I

The Wave

Same reason

Different direction

Stasis

I ask nothing

And give all

For what is love

And love, life

But cages unlocked

The absence of self?

Away

I am here

A signpost on the road

Valiant-for-Truth

Pointing the way

Guiding, guarding

To what you want

That which you need

The Wave

Then, as always

I am here

And you

Will be there

Waters Fall

Rain falling

Dancing, to earth

Its rhythm, beat

Not the measure

Of the drums of man

But as shifting

Winds through leaves

The heartbeat

Of the world

Songs of the Heart

I could play you a song

Send you the words

The Wave

Written by another

Yet I would rather

Give you words, lines

Of my own heart

Though they be

Rough-hewn from stone

Carved in oak and ash

They will be mine

And, then, yours

Each for Equal #IWD2020

In the true nature

Of humankind

None are more

Or less equal

In denying this

We deny ourselves

Unable to see

With our hands

Over our eyes

The Wave

Logos

In the beginning

Was the word

Or so you say

Thus, we are told

Merely slivers

Of the whole

The garden-gate

Barely ajar

Sea foam

On deep oceans

Compartments

I like things in boxes

Clearly named, described

According to form, function

Anatomy, physiology

But this, I cannot

It defies my reason

The Wave

Beyond and above

Any words I could choose

Cannot be explained

To one enquiring

It is what it is

And I am content

With nothing

And with everything

Giving Space

I could see the hurt

Eyes palest blue

The walls, shield, mask

Raised and worn

All pierced my heart

The pain of seeing

Your pain, knowing

Nothing I could do

The Wave

Independence

Out of the blue

They played your song

The timing, perfect

So, I listened

My own words

Seemingly pale

In comparison

Kindness

Always be kind

So the sign said

Kindness is to act

With compassion

Whether it be

A flower and a smile

Words of comfort

The bullet

For the rabid dog

The Wave

Awake

A night of dreams

The veil between

Sleeping, and waking

Tattered, thin

Now, the morning

Seeming less concrete

Not as real as

That which was dreamt

More and more

The two worlds

I stand between

The human and the other

Less and less

Separated, distinct

Messages and meanings

I am yet to divine

The Wave

Moonlight

I cannot lose you

Nor, in turn, gain

For you are never mine

Nor ever will be

Anyone's but your own

Nets thrown to snare

The moon's reflection

Smoke, Fog

A dry bemusement

Observing myself

Trying to grasp

Hold close things

Which cannot, will not

Be possessed

The Wave

Fihi Ma Fihi

I thought it would fade

Disappear if ignored

If I distracted myself

Or remained silent

Yet, here it is

Still, here I am

Apples and Oranges

For so long

Far too long

Have I watched

Them, him, chosen

Wondering, measuring

Myself against

Seeing only the lack

Of my substance

Worth, and form

Now only I weigh

The Wave

My self against self

A warrior, seer

King amongst men

To What End

In every moment

And all things

Lies the test

And lesson in one

I face the joys

And the sorrows

As equal, knowing

They are sunlight, water

For my soul

Beholder

Seeing you

Sunlit hair

Eyes blue

The Wave

As the sky

We talked

I beheld

Presence

To be here is a given

But to what degree, level

Am I to be present

In type, essence, form

Neither too much

Nor to be too little

Adjusting moment to moment

What you want and need

As much, if not more

Than that I desire

To stand on the bridge

Between, under, heaven

The Wave

The Living Ocean

I would rather ride the waves

Till they break on the shore

The soaring peaks, crests

Down to abyssal troughs

Taste the salt, air to breathe

The urgency of the storm wild

Sense, know, to live

Than the be becalmed

Valentine's Day

If it takes today

For you to feel loved

Then I do not

Deserve you

Be every day

My valentine

The Wave

Kejserens Nye Klæder

There are days when

In word, and verse

Too much is said

And opened window

Revealing all

The emperor disrobed

I know no different

Yet perhaps, should I learn

Suitcase

A long way from home

Again, I realise

The immensity of what is

The nothingness of I

The Wave

Lucky

It's a bittersweet thing

To be here, not there

A part, not the all

One of, but not the

Sitting on the sidelines

An Ode to Tolkien

The board is set

The pieces are moving

We have come to it at last

The great battle of our time

What honour it is

Such fierce joy

To stand

And to fight

The Wave

Fences

The grass is green

Gardens abundant

When tended, fed

Watered, loved

With devotion, care

And attention

But yours is not there

On the other side

It is here, here

What kind of fool

Tends his neighbours field

While his own

Fallow, and barren

Cessation

I lied to myself

That I would write no more

The Wave

Cast the pen away

Leave it by the path

Instead, and again

I picked it up

Held it close

I cannot let it go

As much a part of me

Able to be lost

As my heart or soul

Wages

There is no reward

Worthier than the battle

The flower blooms, falls

Undue

I am my own man

My thoughts and action

Decisions, my own

The Wave

Not yours, theirs

The rewards and blame

Squarely on my shoulders

A Waging of War

I do not know if it is

My head, or my heart

Both, or a something

Somewhere in between

Telling me to call time

To cease this inner war

But, what then

Which side the victor

Neither, or both

To remain, or to go

Walk forward or away

I have not the answers

And thus, I am still

The Wave

Opening

The lock corrodes

An erosion of stone

Hourglass sands

Falling through fingers

I have no time

For time is not

The setting sun

Arises, and again

And I am at peace

Rout

The battle is lost

I held no hope, thought

Of victory, or triumph

Yet still I fought

Still, I fight

Still, I remain

Standing, a man

The Wave

Upright among ruins

7.24am to Central

The carriage is still

While the world rushed past

Air thick, and heavy

The malaise not all due

To the blanket of summer

Eyes downcast, and minds

To devices, to the floor

A race, once proud and noble

Reduced to going here

Then there, for what

Clock on, off, repeat

I do not want this

This, is not me

The Wave

Muted

Instead of pouring

Words on to pages

Instead, silence

Hold it within

Permeate it all

Within, and through

Harness and yoke

Bending it to my will

Know it for what

It is, and is not

20/20 Vision

Hindsight is not clarity

Without dissection, analysis

Of each part

Anatomy and physiology

But clouded still

By perception, judgment

The Wave

Subjective for, against

There can be only

This moment

A story unfolding

In which we all

Can be heroes

If we choose

In the Old Masonic Hall

Sunday comes as if

The night and day are one

Yesterday and tomorrow

One endless moment

A wind, soaring

Over ocean and hill

Through tree, by stone

Without beginning

Without end

The Wave

Salt

Midnight at the water's edge

Where waves endless wash

My heart in the wind

As full as the ocean

Empty as the sky

The Demon Beast Bows Down to the Warrior

By fate, the sword came

Long had it lain

Sheathed, forgotten

Yet its vigil, sharp

I take its name for myself

For blade and I are one

One, my nature

Other, have I become

The Wave

Aft and Fore

Sleepless, turning

Thinking too much

Am I wrong

Have I done ill

Are there debts

Of honour owed

Eyes on wash and wake

Instead of fore

To bow and beyond

Fallen

I don't want to let go

Nor to give up

Neither do I know how

Yet I must before

I am burned to ash

Torn asunder

Drowning without dying

The Wave

There is nothing

For me here

Yet, I remain

Rivers

Of sorrow, I know

And of love

I have followed both

Their waters unto

The springs from

Which they flow

Now I stand on banks

Green, shadowed

Where the two

Course into one

A Rupturing of Levels

It is a strength

And self-destruction

The Wave

Fracturing the sphere

Of the ego, of pride

A letting-go

But not lessening

Tending it closely still

To hear your head

As well as heart

Telling you to open

To what may well be

Breaking the Dry

Night descends and deepens

And with it, the rain

Temper the fevered air

Washing the leaves

Brown and green

A quiet drum rhythm

As the earth breathes in

The Wave

Thursday

There are many things

For which there are no words

Thus, I am rendered mute

To see you unguarded

Masks unneeded, cast aside

The song on your lips

As you dance, free

Sunlight and rains

Of your heart

Freedom

Free will

Is not a right

It is a gift

One to be earned

Through ascesis

Of the spirit

Flesh, and mind

The Wave

Scar

We are not broken

Without choosing

To remain in pieces

Whatever may come

The wounds suffered

Are lessons

Chances to scour away

To find the perfect

The eternal beneath

Cold Turkey

A hard edge

To sight and thought

The cleansing

Blood through veins

Air in lungs

The Wave

Mit Dir, Ohne Dich

Here, not there

Together

Yet apart

Industrial

Darkened waters

Below the bridge

Black among the green

Exam

A simple test of spirit

To do, or do not

There is nothing else

No in between

One, or the other

www.ingramcontent.com/pod-product-compliance
Lightning Source LLC
Chambersburg PA
CBHW070309010526
44107CB00056B/2534